AF268802

LADY OF THE MURALS

Also by Stephen Oliver

Henwise (1975)
& interviews (1978)
Autumn Songs (1978)
Letter To James K. Baxter (1980)
Earthbound Mirrors (1984)
Guardians, Not Angels (1993)
Islands of Wilderness—A Romance (1996)
Unmanned (1999)
Election Year Blues (1999)
Night of Warehouses: Poems 1978-2000 (2001)
Deadly Pollen (2003)
Ballads, Satire & Salt—A Book of Diversions (2003)
Either Side The Horizon (2005)
Parable of The Sea Sponge (2007)
Harmonic (2008)
Apocrypha (2010)
Intercolonial (2013)
Gone: Satirical Poems: New & Selected (2016)
Luxembourg (2018)
Heroides / 15 Sonnets (2020)
The Song of Globule / 80 Sonnets (2020)
Cranial Bunker (2023)
Poems In Retrospect: A Selection (2025)

Prose

Unposted, Autumn Leaves / A Memoir In Essays (2021)

LADY OF THE MURALS
The Prose Poems
2005-2025

STEPHEN OLIVER

GP
GREYWACKE PRESS
Lat. 25°/50° South. Long. 145°/180° East

First published 2026

Greywacke Press
9 Lynch
St Hughes
ACT 2605
Australia
reid1801@bigpond.com
greywackepress@gmail.com

Oliver, Stephen 1950-
Title: *Lady of The Murals: The Prose Poems*
ISBN 9 781764 533706

Cover design composed by Stephen Oliver
Photo: Margaret Muir / Trig-Station Hill, Hamilton East

Affinity formatting by John Denny
of Puriri Press, Auckland

A catalogue record for this book is available
from the National Library of Australia

Acknowledgements

These prose poems, some revised, are taken from the following collections: Nos: 1-14, *Either Side The Horizon*, Titus Books, Auckland (2005); Nos: 15-34, *Luxembourg*, Greywacke Press, Canberra (2018); Nos: 35-60, *Cranial Bunker*, Greywacke Press, Canberra (2023); Nos: 61-70, *new & previously unpublished* (2025).

Vive La Sans-Dents (39) shortlisted for the *Fair Australia Poetry Prize* (2019).

The Anthropolite Man (15) republished in *The Australian Prose Poem Anthology*, edited by Cassandra Atherton and Paul Hetherington, Melbourne University Press (2020).

That Farther Shore (48) I.M. Rudi Krausmann (1913-2019), translated into German by Heinz. L. Kretzenbacher. Original English & German translation republished in *Poetry Sydney* (2024).

Lady Of The Murals (40), title prose poem of this collection, originally published in *Verity La* Australia, and subsequently republished along with many of these prose poems in *Poems In Retrospect: A Selection*, Greywacke Press, Canberra (2025).

'The poetical language of any age should be
the current language heightened'
—*Gerard Manley Hopkins*

Contents

1. A COUNTRY MILE — 3

2. EMBLEM — 4

3. CONTAINING A BROKEN COLUMN — 5

4. MAPPING THE TERRAIN — 6

5. INTERSECTION — 7

6. INDUSTRIAL TABLEAU — 8

7. TO FEED A MOCKINGBIRD — 9

8. MORNING SENDS THE HEART SOARING — 11

9. PRELUDE TO A TIME MACHINE — 12

10. THE HOME AS HOMICIDE — 13

11. CONFESSIONS OF A GENETICIST — 14

12. TO THE FLOATING ISLES — 15

13. DIVINING PAEKAKARIKI — 16

14. *mal de mer*—IN SEARCH OF THE GODS — 18

15. ANTHROPOLITE MAN — 19

16. TRACKING RUPERT BROOKE — 20

17. APOCRYPHA — 22

18. BAKED POTATO — 23

19. THE TRANSFORMATION — 24

20. OPEN-LEARNING WORKSHOPS — 25

21. THE VENDORS — 31

22. COCKAIGNE — 32

23. THE GREAT ROGATUS — 33

24. SLOW RELEASE — 34

25. JACOB'S LADDER — 35

26. ELECTRICIAN — 36

27. THE JOURNEY — 38

28. DARK MATTER — 39

29. CHORISTERS — 40

30. BLACK SWANS — 41

31. BROKEN — 42

32. YELLOW CHEVRONS — 43

33. DOMES — 44

34. TESTAMENT — 45

35. MANIFEST — 46

36. BANISHMENT — 47

37. VISITANT — 49

38. THE LITERALIST — 50

39. VIVE LA SANS-DENTS — 51

40. LADY OF THE MURALS — 52

41. STAMP MILL — 53

42. OTHERWISE — 54

43. THE BRASHER DOUBLOON (1947) — 55

44. GO THE DISTANCE — 56

45. THE COMMON GOOD — 57

46. BIG DATA — 58

47. FOREST OF STARS — 59

48. THAT FARTHER SHORE — 60

49. THE POLITICIAN — 62

50. ANTHONY KINGSMILL-LUNN (1926-1993) — 63

51. THE PRINTER — 65

52. DIGITAL GHOSTS — 66

53. FARTHER OFF — 67

54. BURN DOWN THE AMAZON — 68

55. FANDANGO — 69

56. OBLIGATORY — 70

57. OSSUARY   71

58. REBRANDED FREEDOM   72

59. ENACTED ELSEWHERE   73

60. PHANTOMS   74

61. LETTERS TO THE LOST   75

62. THE BIG BLUE BULL   76

63. AN AWAKENING   78

64. SPUN FREE   79

65. FLICKERING COMPASS   80

66. LYING LOW   81

67. HERMIT'S CELL   82

68. LAKESIDE   83

69. GRAND REHEARSAL   84

70. HIS BELIEF   85

LADY OF THE MURALS

A COUNTRY MILE

Consider the *Lilies of the Field*. Amongst landmines in Afghanistan, Bosnia, Eritrea, Ethiopia, Mozambique, Angola, Cambodia, and Egypt—which tops the bill with twenty three million landmines. Wherever invading troops in retreat have left a tidal slick of bone fragment, gobbets of flesh, stumps that were once children, old men, women. Limbs vaporized.

Landmines Must Be Stopped campaigns the UN. A small girl in a bright dress picking up a shiny object. The dress made brighter. Consider the *Lilies of the Field*, the exploding blooms of landmines, so spectacularly undramatic, a muffled bang, a puff of smoke and dirt, from the safe distance of a news clip. Untidy air.

But on a winter's night, bare branches before a rushing sky. A turbulent moon. The earth smelling black, breathing, holding in these subcutaneous cysts, metal implants, each a footpad for the crazy dance of death. Millions of them (est. twenty years to clear at current rate) each with its own graven serial number, endlessly patient, waiting the impress of heel, or lightly shifting step.

This light over the land, made ancient by earlier habitations, wars, villages and migrations, dismantling through the hours and days, over long stretches of time; minefields—abandoned tracts of land. *The Lilies of the Field* so secure in their fate that every spring they bloom here, as though announcing entrance to the cemetery and underworld.

EMBLEM

The hen is not so wise, nor *Zbigniew Herbert* skewered. Asbestos coloured, squat soldier of understorey and tree base, neurotic inhabitant of the tribal village, rhomboid citizen of backyards that no longer exist, behind hill-perched, stuccoed houses affronting panoramic harbour views. Zany monitor of daybreak, escapee to macrocarpa and rafter, beyond the precincts of wire netted fowl runs.

A squabble of hens is unparliamentary, a ruck and scrummage, an embodiment of what a crowd is; a potential riot. A motley of tribes and tongues, a disorder of nations, barrio and ghetto inhabitant. A bloom of feathers overriding reptile claws, milliner's folly, tavern sign, a disposition at odds with itself, grounded, clumsy amongst branches, its awareness a half-remembered flight. Avian refugee. Progenitor of griffin.

We are thus related to this fallibility—a half complete species; two parts absurdity, one part dream. Served up at an evolutionary banquet of invention and ferocious self-consumption.

CONTAINING A BROKEN COLUMN

It is likely given the salty taste of this first line the lake reached this far up the cliff face, and that these dinosaur prints—set in the rock like official seals to a document of great geological import, will not disclose a world once existent on a vertical plane—merely one where time stretched its bones upward when the world was a little more malleable, its joints plastic, and given to immensely large gestures.

When the world was, in fact, complete and primordial, not the collection of genetic left overs, odds and ends it is today, cats-eye marbles blindly rolled before the sacrificial altar of science, under 'the old star eaten blanket of the sky'.

> Eglantine wreathes this basalt
> stone, temple remnant, that might
> have held a bust to its God,
> celebrant of harvest, protector of
> fleets, guardian of homeland and
> hearth, his gaze directed westward
> toward *The Garden of the Hesperides*.

We commemorate our first experiments in the Temple of Genetics as we remembered our original evolutionary mutations on Notre Dame and on the great medieval cathedrals of Europe. Religion naturally prefigured these creations as demonic, but Hell can not exist because it is the absence of memory.

It is this loss which constitutes the horror. Each of our inventions becomes, in effect, not a confirmation of progress, but a valediction, a remembering back to a time when the thicket in the forest was not a dark dream—that point at which fear created the sacred, the illusory world in which we move today.

MAPPING THE TERRAIN

A long car, a black night, tail lights push the bulk slowly round the slow curve of a hill, and blur. An indeterminate colour like a thought suspecting itself. A CEO has just been wiped off by a diminutive PA. His mobile pulses, snaps aquamarine. A trophy home, or is that an observatory ahead? The great dome of the sky swings open but no finger, points. No electrical charge of touch, that says, 'To exist is okay'.

The plaited lights of the city like the weave in an Aztec fabric, or heavy chest adornment thrown down in haste. Brilliant beads, trailing a brilliant wetness of multi-colour. Abrupt as a blow to the back of the head. Death: a memorable amnesia. Somehow, it must be like that, *as Arthur Koestler foresaw it*, the slow and invisible thump of a drum away in the distance, felt more as pulse than heard. Passing across chrome, the city smeared glitz as the limo stretches toward the ridge. An instant before The Fall, that point at which death was invented. God's perfect pal hurled down from the heavenly ramparts. The shattering realization of loss whose brushed aside light, that every night, is reaching out to us still.

INTERSECTION

The secret lies in elevation; in the erection of it, its meaning, what it relates to. The concept of the finite gave way to loss. Dream gave way to prophecy. Clearing the plains of primordial forest invited perspective. *The finite, elevation, loss, perspective.* These are the fundamental ingredients that define homage. Stone is the vehicle for homage, because stone represents elevation and irredeemable time; it is a man-made contrivance in the spirit of permanency, an acknowledgement of absence.

The analytical axe split the proposition in two: material—shamanic. Exactly what is lost cannot be known because absence simultaneously suggests replacement. A tree is replaced by a standing stone. A bush thicket becomes a hut, the moment of destruction is the moment of discovery, orgasm is death, violence and sex, etc. Loss, however, is immeasurable because it is boundless. Loss accretes over time into mythology.

The metaphysician slowed, paused at the lights. In the car opposite (to his left) a blonde with a Nordic profile gripped the steering wheel like a seafarer gripping the tiller in an Atlantic sea squall. Her eyes, unambiguous as a theodolite, calibrated the coordinates from point, to the shopping-strip four intersections distant. Her knuckles that whitened on the steering wheel indicated a life of vigorous, dominant sex. Her tensed form, crouched over the dashboard reminded him of the trebuchet, sprung, at the moment of release. He was at least five hundred years and one continent out in his appreciation of this woman.

INDUSTRIAL TABLEAU

What lies at the end of this petrol-hued rainbow, is an oil-slick way out to sea, overarching proboscis sucking up light and colour into bands, into a glorious stain of creation. The refinery port of Botany Bay could be Piraeus, Jaffa or Tel Aviv. Flat-land horizon, reminiscent of an earlier, grandfatherly generation.

Gasworks and pylons, steam trains chugging between the first and second world wars under sooty railway bridges, beneath a cloth cap sky. The pit-head wheel stilled, the first and last grotto of the Industrial Revolution. In these narrow regions, asphalt fades grey in back streets, rail yards blur into rust and weed. Lime oxidises in abandoned brick yards. The solitary coal stacks stand sentinel at dusk. The final, romantic tableau.

Summer is sustained, momentary, and present. Car-sized concrete blocks pack the breakwater. White storage tanks glisten tidily, compose to view the fuel depot. Small waves dissolve into miniature cornices and cartouches upon the sand. Whittled light silvers the waters at Little Bay / La Perouse.

TO FEED A MOCKINGBIRD

In the low lying patches of the exhibition space, over puddles, pieces of broken paint. Stuck on bushes (seen from the viewing area) a flail of gilt-like papyri flecks, as if blown from a terra cotta jar, suddenly opened after 2000 years. Or a gloriously exploded window display, an autumn catalogue suggestive of David Jones, Harrods, Bloomingdales. Yet shocking as a terrorist blast of church glass.

A galaxy of butterfly wing fragments. An impossible Ming Mosaic. Mosque ceramic of spilling fountains and heavenly gardens. A banquet oriental and wafer thin in torn, tremulous, bits. An exhibit at the Indianapolis Zoo of spectacular butterflies; exotic, rare species, consumed by a mockingbird. Lone predator. Thief at dawn. Over a two week spell, avoiding capture, consumed a banquet of diminishing returns. A fabled feast. An alchemy of slow horror. Uninvited guest to a resplendent menu:

(*Heliconius sara*) Small Blue Grecian, (*Agraulis vanillae*) Gulf Fritillary, (*Anartia jatrophae*) White peacock, (*Ascia monuste*) Great Southern White, (*Asterocampa celtis*) Hackberry, (*Asterocampa clyton*) Tawny Emperor, (*Battus philenor*) Pipevine Swallowtail, (*Euptoieta Claudia*) Variegated Fritillary, (*Eurema Lisa*) Dainty Sulphur, (*Eurytides marcellus*) Zebra Swallowtail, (*Limenitis archippus*) Viceroy, (*Nympjalis antiopa*) Mourning Cloak, (*Papilio polyxenes*) Black Swallowtail, (*Phoebis philea*) Orange-barred Sulphur, (*Pterourus palamedes*) Palamedes Swallowtail, (*Urbanus proteus*) Long-tailed Skipper, (*Venessa atalanta*) Red Admiral, (*Venessa virginiensis*) American Painted Lady, (*Caligo artreus*) Owl Butterfly, (*Caligo eurilochus*) Forest Mort Blue, (*Caligo memnon*) Giant Owl Butterfly, (*Heliconius charitonia*) Zebra Longwing, (*Heliconius doris*) Doris Butterly, (*Heliconius era-to*) Crimson Patch Longwing, (*Heliconius hecale*) Golden Helicon, and (*Marpesia petreus*) Ruby Dagger Wing.

In the days that followed this calamity, and after the Associate Press had, according to the principles of the chaos theory (that a butterfly beating its wings in the Northern Hemisphere will cause a storm out in the Indian Ocean) flashed this story around the globe—a spokesperson from the Indianapolis Zoo remarked, 'Our bird could have dined on any of these, but he did seem to have a particular taste for the "Blue Morphos"—a beautiful, large, and slow-flying tropical species.' The mockingbird was taken far away beyond the outskirts of the city and released. Presumably home, at last.

MORNING SEND THE HEART SOARING

Sydney on a Tuesday morning, early September. Spring clangs in—Egyptian distances toward Botany Bay. Fuel haze and aircraft aswim. The season of *petro sunrises* begins. Birds study a new notation, a register higher. Suburban trees pay homage to buildings, puff into lantern green leaf and bud. Jasmine bloom wraiths a driveway, lays its scent over the boundary, tracking the pavement.

Word play between couples ease and relax, assured as an unfinished novel. Each heart a vignette. Speech not yet a song as eyes loft lightward. A clump of wind fusses amongst tree crowns, troubled stillness. A midden of pigeons rise and expand, shell bright against a white, backwash sky. Youth is green as an Elizabethan sward, laughter local as a hedgerow.

Garbage bins release their odours and overflow; little storage silos that make good pickings for the hunched vagrant, selective in the morning traffic, delicately fingering at elbow length breakfast discards. Street noise friable as asphalt. News bulletins rummage amongst the world's dross.

PRELUDE TO A TIME MACHINE

Tin goods sheds, the cantilevered skyline reconfigure throughout the day, the airport busy as a pavement. From here it's twenty four hours in the air to the Northern Hemisphere; older foundations, battle thick walls, multi-layered atmospheres, studded and embossed. One regime after another—history's gargantuan form from whose '*rybes they make bows to shoot with*'. Sheep graze the old battlefields pretty as a picture, amongst the hawthorn and pylons.

Looking south toward Botany Bay, sinking beneath long rooflines, planes drift a bright tail fin along the east-west runway, or suddenly appear before you stuck on the sky like in a child's drawing, cushioned on volumes of engine roar, big colours loading the foreground, movement that is the elongated removal of time in the lifting sweep, diminuendo to a quiet speck, climbing out over the ocean—silvered shafts from a yeoman's bow falling far off to become traffic somewhere.

The mind says that memory is filtered through gauze. And immediately you are there. Banked up yellow soil-rubble along the coastline toward Jaffa Port, fuel storage depot tabernacled in the Mediterranean light, winding through the dockside at Piraeus, (backstreets of Newtown reminiscent of *Ano Petralona*) and the air sweet with petroleum. The day shimmering in youthful heat.

THE HOME AS HOMICIDE

The magnolia flower bruise-purple, cream cupped, under September. Long haul promise of summer heat and forests illuminated in scripts of flame, the sky's pinafore a blue, bleached out migraine.

The land insisting upon its climactic heritage beyond the roar of air conditioning in a million suburban homes, within the short term memory loss of kitchen and living room; discrete zones for the petty crimes of the heart. Clearing rooms for hoarded angers given over to street cred.

Clouds troop from the southern horizon, lightning lays down its picket fence through the postal zones. *Hamid* pulls up alongside *Zang Wei* in the slow lane, and pumps a crescent of bullets into the driver's seat. Intersection lights-gone-yellow-gone-red-gone-green. High season of Taxi Wars along the Princes Highway. The Channel Ten Eye in the Sky helicopter reports traffic backed up to Bankstown.

Follow the metallic serpent with scales flashing back down Parramatta Road to Rockdale. Tomorrow a dawn of middle eastern appearance will rise over Newtown: Gateway to the East.

Sydney, September 10, 2002

CONFESSIONS OF A GENETICIST

Endless time and we with every other thing that ever was. Genesis is a cough. It doesn't matter whether God exists or not, given all the information that we are buried in, what we wade through, like trappers caught out in a blizzard.

Dead or alive, it hardly matters one way or another. Makes small difference in the end—that end for which each and every one of us has his sealed orders, choice of exits, caravanning over days and roads sunlit, snowbound, squally, rain black asphalt—its tongue over the horizon. We squint into the cartoon of our lives amidst fabulous dialogues. No faith will tell us that we are the sum of our inventions, represent nothing more outside the balloon of our own expanding light.

Each copulation promises extension of memory. Each moment of oblivion a biological passport to the genetic code in the perpetual cycle of reproduction. The endless variations we impose upon structures that house existences is the profound exploration of internal organs.

We extrapolate visceral components into paradigms of civilization, mechanisms to trigger other mechanisms. *Esprit de corps.* Having unravelled both the gut's sleepy coils and the brain's walnut circuitry, we are as close to mortality as ever we were. None the wiser and still unmemoried. We flash on an image over and over—that as small children on a voyage of uncertain destination, we saw one glowing cabin window through the fleeting nightfall, and tall tree trunks moving very fast before it, for what seemed like miles upon miles.

Autumn is chequered as a flannel shirt. Folk here are at home in the river valleys that make wide, swinging turns. The big rivers and the big mountains. *Look, Stranger,* on these islands now nothing leaps to view but goats if you get in close enough, (like) on a chopper-shoot out through plateaux and orchilla lichens purpling terrain. A swirl of black and white bobs and dapples over the high country's oxidate palette. Monumental river boulders piled up like hulks in a car wrecker's yard.

Once the earth's axis tilted and shifted, stretching the global latitudes like a hair net. The gods relocated to foreign regions, created a few disordered landmasses along the way. Climates ran hot and cold. Tropical fauna unfolded. Glaciers like herds of unicorn reared, and retreated. Any god's guess as to which way was up. The world, an undiscovered psychic garden, lay in wait.

Not surprisingly, such sentiments are anathema to the 'Rio Earth Summit' repeat performances, the 'Kyoto / Montreal Protocols', the 'World Summit On $ustainable Development' (W$$D). 'Our World Is Not For Sale' enviro-activists fulminate against an immoveable corporate mind set, and its insistence upon greed and greenwash.

Traceries may yet be found in bestiaries, compendiums on forgotten mythologies and migrations. Like any act of faith discovery is mostly guesswork. *"I'd rather go to a country where melancholy means something more than emptiness struggling with itself."* Dimly heard, stranger, in deepest sleep.

DIVINING PAEKAKARIKI

Stitched through the collar of hills from Pukerua Bay to Paekakariki, run five short vintage tunnels built in 1886 (the bore from Pukerua Bay's steep descent to Paekakariki at sixty four feet, qualifies as the shortest on the Main Truck Line) from which the Kapiti Coast opens out to the horizon at extended intervals as a blue-grey (according to the season) or greenly thrashed sea, before another tunnel momentarily swallows the few carriages and the view fifty four metres beneath, adjacent to State Highway 1.

I knew a painter who once considered painting every rail station from Wellington to Paekakariki as an allegorical representation of 'The Stations of The Cross': *Kaiwharawhara, Takapu Road, Redwood, Tawa, Linden, Kenepuru, Porirua, Paremata, Mana, Plimmerton, Pukerua Bay, Muri*. The *Via Dolorosa* working to timetable.

Did he envisage the Christ face hanging over *Ngauranga Gorge* a stand in for Calvary, maybe? The Anglo-Celtic and Northern European mind homages a deity of granite not sandstone. Colder zones where folk are inclined to hibernate indoors for extended wintry periods with their cattle engenders a dour God, breeds a ruminant, obsessive sensibility. The long dark months are better suited to the pagan deities, tangled winds and hours wholly attuned to erratic Godly humours. Christ, after all, is of Middle Eastern appearance, the heart's lone terrorist.

How the metaphor invariably claims the high moral ground. Kapiti Island, a long trestle table lavishly decked out in the Great Reception Room of the Tasman, each point of the compass a turning, rectangular window, bright circular cloud crowning the island's highest peak, forecasting pentecostal rain-sweeps along the coast.

I knew a man who waited upon a tsunami (the caldera around *Krakatau* rumoured, seismically) but the promised great wave never came. He had rolled up his trouser bottoms, stacked box upon box of books, racks of paintings, ready to load up at a moment's buckling of the horizon. His bach at *Wellington Road* remained undisturbed, perched high and dry on old sand dunes, presided over by the Paekakariki hills. Macrocarpa and cabbage tree took to the clefts as expected. Precipitous. The express train came and went daily, the bells clanged over Beach Road Crossing, and the pilgrim poets, writers and artists came and stayed—just as they had done for decades.

If you do not remember yourself in death, mesmerized under the pendulum of that sea, would you care who remembered you after? The visionary demands absences. *Make it your own—you'll remember*. Give uncertainty name and form, fashioned after your inconsistencies, as the Ancients did to make their gods, or as the gods allowed them.

Power to destroy denotes an independent existence, the force to overrule breath, decides fate. So the mythic infrastructure was set in place and materialism became subservient to it. *Vision transmuted into form. Structure duly paid homage*. In time and beyond it, the idea predominated and became the absolute.

The argument: how to reconcile the gods with the one. This became the obelisk set in the technology landscape. Technological invention enveloped the globe in an artificial dimension. The elements of time and space cavorted in the re-enactment of the genesis principle. Chaos is the theory that insists creation equals destruction.

The philosopher's job is to record the progress of enlightenment syllogistically. The poet's job is to preserve memory under the articles of self-effacement.

ANTHROPOLITE MAN

They wore thick leather jerkins. I can't recall the colour, oak brown, or maybe black. The men lumbered like some slow choreographed minstrel show (or mediaeval procession), with giant sacks slung over their backs (bent) round the back of our place to dump the broken load in the cut down packing case that served to house the heaped up coal. The coal man, sometimes two in single file, stooped, heavy stepped, in foul weather or fine, past our kitchen window. Year in year out they filed by, to feed the wetback coal range, which like some leviathan at home in its bay, occasionally breached, sending a spume of steam hissing and bubbling angrily from the roof overflow pipe, only to subside and exhale with a repeated, regurgitant, gasping. Taciturn, stolid men. I dared not speak to them, but only saw their hunched forms on a migratory track they could not seemingly be deflected from. The Anthropolite Man who lived amongst the seams in a world of gleaming, oily shale, tattooed maybe with fronds and ferns from extinct tropical forests, in spirals that could no longer be deciphered.

Had he stayed longer, one could easily have imagined Rupert Brooke strolling down the country roads and lanes of the North Island of New Zealand, an Edwardian in an otherwise Victorian South Pacific country, knocking the heads off dandelions with a switch, but given that he stayed a mere two desultory weeks, more by default than anything else, this is not possible. He was, after all, a man in a hurry, and—though perhaps only half realized at the time—he did have a war to get to. An early, mid-summer morning in the country.

Let us assume Rupert's sensibilities were wistfully inclined, directed toward an English rural setting; before him, as if in the mind's eye, he might have seen: *'At seven o'clock the new risen sun, bursting through the oak leaves, made a perfect spider's web of silver rays. Sky and earth were misty. The grass-blades and bramble leaves were dewy grey, the dandelion clocks were all over diamonds, at the edge of the dusty road: the elderberry bunches hung heavy and drenched above them.'*

Just as Edward Thomas described it in his essay, London Miniatures. But this was not his England, or anybody else's. Rupert had bade farewell to his hosts, the Studholmes of Ruanui Station located just out of Taihape, where he had stayed for a few days, and who on his request may have dropped him on the outskirts of this small country town where he was happy enough to walk the mile or so to the Taihape train station (even though his foot, poisoned in Fiji, continued to trouble him a little) to catch the Wellington Express, and there to take a boat in a few days time to Tahiti on his return to England, and then on to his final destination—the imminent, first world war.

The country was troubled by strikes and he considered the women if not ugly certainly dowdy. While waiting for the train he angrily scribbled free form poems about the death of beauty and love's demise. In disgust he stuffed the crumpled notepaper into a hole in the station waiting room wall. The hole had been made by a violent kick from a working class boot. These poems would have revolutionized modern poetry. They were never found.

APOCRYPHA

Fog percolates through inaccessible valleys. *A mackle-faced moon.* Lyricism is a herd of goats that scatters into the bush line. No precipitate ridge-to-ridge leaping here. This is not ancient Greece, (the Greece in thrall to its gods) and certainly, not Europe. It is a dream of mediaeval cartographers. This is the southernmost archipelago; a largely temperate climate, and memoried by a handful of glaciers, white wolves retreating into an alpine landscape. No one lives here. There exists moss, forest, dripping fern, and tussock. This is its language, but because no one lives here the language has never been spoken. Even the suburbs stand empty like some failed dream of the unarrived. Houses are a handful of croutons thrown over lumped up hills. As if the Great Confectioner, in one moment of joyous release, flung from his palm little cubes of manna. It is understandably very sad, and much like a journey never taken.

BAKED POTATO

I take a bright kitchen knife, spear the baked potato from the oven, dry parchment rasp and pop, transfer to my dinner plate, then with a serrated little black-handled knife I saw down the middle, the potato steams and rustles. A Sybil's grotto. Gasps its doughy breath. Then I cram in sour cream with a little butter, salt & black pepper grainy as beach sand. A votive offering. Then as I regard this construction, it falls open like a bible, tells tales to my tongue and palate; taste of fields, and memory of farms once measured by the chain; of morning mists rising over the stark and ghostly skeletons of poplars. Wagon wreck by the barn door, the barn with disheveled loft. One barn owl. A scythe blade sharpened on the edge of the moon. Munitions hidden in heavy sacks of barley grain. This cautionary tale from the plosive potato slumped in the middle of my white dinner plate. Still and steaming, fresh as a cowpat on a shiny autumn morning, bleeding in its pool of sour cream with a little butter.

THE TRANSFORMATION

Light decides knuckled contours, capturing loss that catches us all out in the end. We observe this singular moment—such epiphany led men out into the desert. The soft-pronged leaf of the Olive branch found on Classical pottery, the Greeks, then Romans, circled each other for honours with their conflicting and merging gods. Amphorae. Before this articulated stand off, a desert people configured the image as menorah. First light of moon glazed around pottery, under a slow and revolving sky. Silence sheering off into blackness and pricked light. Pressure on the eardrums the hermit knew. Eternal listening. Clay thrown wetly on the potter's wheel. The olive branch, how it lifts up its soft-pronged candelabra against the rain, and then—see how it turns, silvers.

Advice to a novelist

Supply the characters of the story with a set of travel-brochures, then let them talk amongst themselves. NB: Your characters must always be vastly more intelligent than you are. This puts you immediately above critical notice. Buy a sheep dog and avoid blondes at cocktail parties. A sober, disgruntled approach to the reading public is advisable. Short bursts of articulate invective highly recommended. Take up darts.

Advice to a poet

Don't take the whole business too seriously. Adopt long distance walking as a hobby. Don't become a typographical cowboy or you will be mistaken for a signwriter. Guard against becoming a funambulist sans balancing pole. Failure means you are one step away from becoming a successful copywriter. Success means you are one step closer to never having to write another lousy word.

Advice to a playwright

Invite all those detestable people in your circle to first night. Then leave alone by taxi for the nearest nightclub. This will prepare you for the morning review notices. Structure your dialogue as you would a scaffold: vocal pictographs around an imagined community of individuals. Discard long monologues about the world gone to hell. All people want to do is get home safely. The more avant-garde your play the better, the audience loves nostalgia. Acts are for the apostles.

Advice to a landscape painter

Ignore the existing mytho/historical landscape which you have either inherited, or migrated to. You are Adam. Nothing can be created without the imposition of your unique will. Size is important and affirms to the viewer's eye that you are a monumentalist in breadth and neo-classicist in scope. They fail to see that you are a dedicated billboard artist. One day you will move to Las Vegas.

Advice to a linguist

Language? Hardly. Hair bound words slavering at the mouth's cave. Speech clubbed to falsehood. Why is this so? Listen to production's moist purr that blocks the way back. To where? No sacred groves remain to ask in. Get a job as a taxi driver in a third world country. Storerooms are regarded as primordial, sacred places.

Advice to an English Lecturer

Your future lies with the private sector. Stage dinner parties for book reviewers. Court publishers as your intermediate friends. Start up a literary magazine with an east European bias and nominate yourself as a cultural commissar. This is your birthright. Push post-structuralist theory through other writers. Culture = Power = Exclusivity. You are a cultural supremacist whose root cause is self-loathing in the knowledge you lack originality. Join the local Press Club.

Advice to a philologist

Converse with tramps. Record the patois of those who prefer to live under viaducts as opposed to living in storm water drains. For a location guide consult your local government sponsored unemployment centre. Avoid detention camps. The language of the tin cup tapped out on bars in high security prisons is central to your understanding and visualizing primitive speech patterns. Read George Borrow's *Lavengro*. Move into a housing estate.

Advice to a medievalist

Lecture Notes: Catholic church as living reliquary of medievalism. Opulence continues to flagrantly contradict each new interpretation of modernism and contemporary thought. Catholic authority prevails as anachronism. The last stand of medieval land baron mentality in a virtual world. The monastic spirit is long dead. Universities have sworn fealty to the Corporates. Become an itinerant scholar qua goliard.

Advice to a web designer

You are the modern equivalent of the sandwich board man and the world is your pavement. You carry with you shop frontages of all the cities of the world. When you advertise, 'Eat at Joe's' you create a global franchise. Each window you design is a card plucked from fortune's pack. Your credo: everything and nothing has value, the world is a pixelated glass ball.

Advice to a biographer

Your job is to compress time so that personal incident in the life you are reporting on becomes an historical event. This permits you to make logically imagined links in the disordered chronology that is an individual's life. Elevate a life to the level of the subject's recorded achievements. You must disguise the fact that you are merely an officially sanctioned gossip. Your quandary is that fact gets in the way of opinion.

Advice to a language poet

You have recurrent dreams of a ticker tape parade on Wall Street. You are showered by your own compositions. Millions of letters and symbols. This dream symbolizes your endless capacity to promulgate disinformation and untruth. The greater the abstraction the greater your success. Obscurantism equals originality which is, nevertheless, a borrowed concept. You are a social media terrorist and disciple of SoundCloud, or whatever comes next. Infinity is a manageable excursus.

Advice to a Book Review editor

One day you will be taken seriously. Meantime, you remain the stooge of book barn syndicates. What author you promote will decide guest appearances at literary festivals, Hyatt Hotel book launches, et al. Safety lies in numbers. Affect an intellectual stance in the manner of film critic to secure regular, weekly spots on National Radio and Sunday Morning TV Talk Shows. You plan one day to become 'reviewer in residence' at a leading American Creative Writing School.

Advice to a literary festival director

You are, in essence, the grand puppeteer, politician of the highest bureaucratic order. You must be seen as the non-partisan dispenser of the public purse. Knights Templar of popular, belles-lettres. Spend your days and nights in the off season shifting through flowcharts and sales figures from multinational, publishing companies in order to make a selection of authors. Beware the 'margin call'.

Advice to a Literary Agent

Your job is to find a publisher for anything that can be written down and sold. Creativity and originality are the least of your concerns. Publishing is a whorehouse, you are the pimp, your clients the pampered customers. You belong to an elite guard promulgating unbridled consumerism and conspire with multinational publishing houses to lock up the market under the motto: Whoever Sells Wins. Treat every Ms as a potential film script. Your success like every agent lies in bulk billing.

Advice to a Poetry Society

You manage a glorified canteen for itinerant writers and a trash & treasure market for informal reading venues. As an amateur organization that aspires to the trappings of the prestigious literary luncheon you are, at your most ambitious, nothing more than an imploding committee in search of an authority. Your salvation lies in bus tours, to and from retirement villages, and as a sideline, promoting Poets in Parks.

Advice to an in-house editor

Grammar is not an issue. Avoid alphabetical lists of first lines and titles as end pages at all costs. In effect, you are a page collator with aspirations toward a doctorate in English Literature and a career based upon your first novel, which remains unwritten. Your job is to look, listen and learn. If you work for a low-ranked academic press, pander to your publisher, who is basically an unqualified sub-editor with no, or little understanding of original poetics, beyond the current, clichéd fashion. Study Kindle and ebook returns. Do not publicly cultivate the company of writers. Vote Labour.

Advice to a geneticist

Change your hairstyle to traditional '50s short back 'n' sides, or military buzz cut. Avoid corduroy and similar fustian wear in favour of ersatz loafers and chinos. Join a mock combat group for weekend macho bonding sessions in the bush. Write a long narrative sonnet sequence on neural transmitters, titled, Blameless Memories. Quote J.B.S. Haldane and Professor A.N. Whitehead at every opportunity. Read David Lodge for relaxation during long international flights. Subscribe to the Icelandic Genome Quarterly. Write a paper on The Inherited Semiotic Characteristics of the Y Chromosome. Secure an invite to Icelandic seminars as speaker on a yearly basis. Stand as Independent for your community.

Advice to a young poet

Every thought is an act of translation. Translation is the act of sympathetic betrayal. Poetry is the act of memory and truthful record pays homage to it. The literary critic is the foreign agent in the camp. His job is to encode untruth and misinformation. His is the art of contradiction passed off as informed judgement. He is in league with the fashionable clique of the day. Know this and secure faith in your own poetic survival—if for no more than one revelatory moment.

THE VENDORS

It was only upon reflection. The glimpse suggested light welling up from the darkness of the stormwater drain had shifted his orientation. All the translucent icicles melted so that what lay before him was indefinable as grey sludge. The monitor into which he gazed, a digital crystal bowl, only gave back to him a myriad of distractions at any one time. These annulled every question he might have asked had he understood the need for one. As if an answer were necessary to his investigation. But what might this disclose?

Images and banners passed before him in procession over the plains of the monitor like a mediaeval pageant or armies on the move. Then he realized it was nothing more than the market-place rabble. Vendors selling their wares silently as if in a mime. Only at the farthermost stalls, on the outer circle, could be heard the sound of something abandoned as though an echo had bounced and broken. He knew then agitation as movement had replaced focus. There was little danger—for the crowd would not cohere and no one sought common purpose. As long as he held onto this one notion he knew that retreat into something he had forgotten was possible.

COCKAIGNE

The hydrologists were unanimous—not all rivers flowed to the sea. Many had stalled. River mouths and estuaries silted. The mightiest of them grown sluggard (the river in a coffin) inched in eddies, trending sou'west, opened its palm arthritically to the sea. Transmontane systems yet made a show of it, garbled through gravel, under bridges, pushed coastward. There were no 'rivers great and fine / of oil, milk, honey and wine' as heralded by the wandering scholars who laughed loudly at the afterlife.

The unveiling of The Temple of the Sacred Cow, a cacophony of pump and filter, rose twenty storeys chrome bright, over-looked vast river plains to the north, garlands of pennyroyal heaped at its base. Along the horizon, high rise apartment blocks (fallen angels) glowed incandescent into the night as if they had stolen fire from the heavens. What of those river gods and creatures celebrated in bestiaries? Scouting parties of laboratory technicians took samples from tributary and anabranch; found no indicators for marine life, only ample evidence of emptiness.

THE GREAT ROGATUS

He takes our breath away, does Rogatus the Mexican Funambulist, on his highwire strung across the Rio Grande. How confident he is. How audacious! Each elegant footstep placed one in front of the other, just so. He even manages to wiggle his hips for the girls watching, breathless, either side. Look there, emblazoned across the back of his black velvet tunic, 'The Great Rogatus'. *Le Grand Seigneur* of empty air!

He pens love songs in Spanish. 'O my sweet Estrella', he trills, 'my little cake of soap, you attract me stronger than any fridge magnet,' he croons, stepping lightly, 'but you slip too easily from my grasp.' Then he stops. What a show off! With a flourish, produces a bouquet of red roses from his white ruffle shirt, sheds petals into the chasm yawning beneath. The river a meandering, silver thread, shiny as the stitching on his damask slippers.

On he goes stealthy as a police informant. A breath of wind quickens. Not even a lover's gasp can unsettle him now. He will make it, adept as translation into a second language. He dreams that one day, on some small archipelago far, far away he will walk between the Ivory Towers of Academia. He will enrapture everyone. Rogatus the Mexican Funambulist has reached the other side—and not one hair out of place.

SLOW RELEASE

In Manaus, Brazil, the Rubber Barons of the 19th century served champagne to their horses and sent their laundry to Portugal. They imported prostitutes from Europe, and lived a life in imitation of the Bell Époque. Carrara marble, late Renaissance art brought from Italy glowed within these jungle mansions.

The local, rufous skinned Indians worked the plantations for a pittance, driven on by an habitual and 'sustainable' poverty—a V cut groined into the bark of the tree (*Hevea brasiliensis*) allowed the milky latex to drip into buckets at such an impossibly slow rate, you wondered how such vast fortunes could ever have been amassed.

Nevertheless, a laticiferous guarantee of dynasties for the colonists and their imperial industries abroad. This was style and exploitation on a grand scale. Columbus who 'discovered' the Americas in 1492, found Brazil eight years later—first the parley and proffered help, then finally betrayal, that mother of invention, inevitably unfolded.

The steady annihilation of tropical forests followed, just as the human body similarly cut, subsides into death as the blood ebbs from the wrists, and into the tepid bath. The slow release of consciousness, that voyage into the unknown, disclosed sacrifice, shamanistic and conjured.

JACOB'S LADDER

It took ten years. The Rosetta spacecraft finally reached its destination. The European Space Agency (ESA) for whom time is an imperative, initiated a few tricky manoeuvres. Time in space is relative. Rosetta and the comet are now locked in a synchronized dance, one around the other. At its closest point, the craft will come to within 50 km, contingent upon speed and gravitational distortion. High resolution images reveal a duck shaped, tumbling object, an ice cream cake texture, a five kilometre nucleus. Surface temperature averages 70°C. Dark and dusty not (as anticipated) icy and dry. The Philae lander will be deployed once a suitable target site is located. The comet swings in a vast, elliptical orbit between Jupiter and Mars, rushing toward the inner solar system at 55,000 kilometres per hour.

Is there nothing faster than light? Thought is. The comet will tell us what we already know—that the origin of the atomic scale is Jacob's Ladder reaching up into the heavens. Time in space is relative. We listen to an endless oscillation of sound, through immeasurable silences. We seek irrefutable evidence that the human species passed this way light years before.

ELECTRICIAN

The electrician lives in a villa of brown clinker brick with aluminium window frames high on a hill in a new sub-division. Smoky tinted glass. The young wife is seen outside on washing days. Daily, she arranges ornate flowers in white ceramic vases behind those windows. A glory of colour that cannot be seen from the outside. She keeps house. From the lounge ceiling hangs one massive crystal chandelier.

They live high on the hill with other villas which look the same or that represent variations of sameness. The electrician drives to jobs all over the district six days a week in his van burnished bright with signage.

His wife who knows where he is at any given moment empowers him. She has his lunch prepared daily at 12:30: PM sharp. He stares through the smoky glass windows and says nothing or says very little. Nothing more than is necessary. Why invite indecision? The countryside seen through his windows rolls away in soft brown tones throughout the seasons.

In the middle distance, below on the flatlands, the sewage treatment pond reflects early morning light. *Lake Tūtae** to the locals. One row of poplars, as if scrawled in italic, serve as backdrop. Even at this distance it looks like a man-made lake. Further out still, a little more to the west of where he now sits, a limestone plant, steam pumping from its stack, glows whitely at this early morning hour.

At the bottom of the exclusive, hilly sub-division—a short distance into town, the supermarket, barking brand names, bustles with the comings and goings of the townsfolk. The electrician dreams of pylons standing guard over his family and over his domain. They hum to him confidentially. Everything that switches on-or-off is within his jurisdiction.

His forsworn duty is to maintain the flow of electricity to every home and family in the district. The chandelier in his living room burns crystal bright late on into the night. He drives out every morning to meet the call. He drives to save the town from dying.

* 'tūtae' is the Maori word for excrement

THE JOURNEY
for Nicole Sprague

Decades of writing, unacknowledged, did not trouble him. A craftsman. He lived an ordinary life in order to keep his extraordinary mind intact. The family grown and gone. Forty years a merchant on Brooklyn Heights. The business his father started. Sold every variety of antique clock, wall and column, black mantel and kitchen clocks.

Here, time whispered in hushed tones. His wife dead these past five years. An aloneness that announced an end to things. After all this time he finally completed one book of small lyrics.

He locked up his brownstone apartment. With a trunk full of newly printed books, poems that explored the minutiae of light and shadow over clock faces, those small mirrors of divination, he set out by Amtrak to crisscross every State in the Union. For as long as it took to empty the trunk of books.

Sought out libraries in cities and country places—journeyed across open prairies and mountains to find them. Peaceful work done at a leisurely pace. With a knapsack full of books he entered each library and, casually, walked by check out. No one paid him any attention.

An old man with cloth cap and knapsack. Found the poetry section, slid onto the shelf one copy of his book, correctly placed in alphabetical order, then left as quietly and purposefully as he came. All across America. Then he went back to the brownstone, unacknowledged, and died.

DARK MATTER

The white moon, a wild mare, driven into the canyon, clouds churned beneath its hooves; toadstools in pine plantations accumulate, some grubby little act performed late at night; green and crinkled, the sheep-terraced hills, white and pink, the purple magnolia bloom.

One singular, brick chimney stack rigid as any branding iron, silent as an exclamation mark. The orbiting, ghost of a house. Beneath and through a copse of native bush, the stream tumbled out of sight, descending into a narrow gorge under the limestone bluff. Looking down from a backcountry road, the whole seen in miniature, suggestive of some pastoral scene not unlike this one. Overall, the sense not of loss but absence.

Once upon a time—but what of it? Nothing happened, no beginnings, endings fizzled out after a few false starts. No discernible joy and even less despair. Nothing happened of any consequence. No fairies at the bottom of the garden, no goblins in the glade.

No agape amongst the livestock; birth and death notices ascended in dizzying columns and as quickly dispersed, like chimney smoke, into nothingness. Dark matter into oblivion. The stream that echoed through the narrow gorge increased and diminished in volume, much as expected, and according to the seasons.

CHORISTERS

Remembered (retrieved) from the Pre-Digital Age as if via virtual wormholes by the loose, chiropractic crack & crunch of spiral carriages shunter-hauled, twisting from one dimension into the next; thought-by-interlocked-thought, the Word propelled through, transfixed, encrypted onto a stelae of stars, hidden behind the Milky Way. *We are the reflection and the mirror, transmission and receptor*, observed the cosmologists. The papal bull declared that theologians, ex-officio, as guardians of mythology, relocate to the Elysium Fields. Here, resided the multitudinous and true gods.

Seen from above through wispy cloud, bomb-churned fields stretched and flickered beneath tinfoil light; it was war. Fear eddied in the eyes of soldiers, and one, though not destined to survive, bore witness. Distilled from this the Gospel of Acedia—fragile as any wan flower discovered within the tank tracks of an advancing column. Oral history would, it was determined, fall to the rumour-mongers. Musicologists, guided by a convocation of choristers, reassembled the broken remnants of song, barely audible, locked within the stone.

BLACK SWANS

IM: Ben Webb

Black swans at Aramoana. The harbour lettuce green as in a watercolour. Otago Peninsula narrowing off Harington Point, and then the open sea. The stately black swans, the running tide. The Spit. A few run down cribs, mostly unoccupied, set back amongst a scattering of pine trees, marram grass and driftwood. Its arm curving out as if to protect itself against the dune forming tides. Early evening in half-light; and suddenly, filling the lounge window at the Pilot's Cottage—bridge and funnel sliding past, massive, in slow motion. The stage machinery turning, dead silent, as though in a waking dream. Perhaps he saw this too, in his last moments, alone in that cottage at The Spit. Focused upon the container ship as it slipped noiselessly out to sea, past Taiaroa Head. What was it then, threw back the image of the terrified child from the dark well? Self-loathing made real in that final act. Afterwards, out there in the darkness, riding upon the waters, black swans arched long velvety necks, and turned toward the dim-lit window with its silhouette, framed there.

BROKEN

For Bob Orr

My brother *Deluxe 1350* portable typewriter. You were at your clattering best back in the '70s, as young as I was, clacked through the days and nights, under wintry, black ribbons of cloud that spooled by, over Reynoldstown high above Careys Bay, up Blueskin Road, toward Mount Cargill. You clattered against nor'westerlies and macrocarpa; clumped windbreaks sloping out across the ridgeline, over rock-strewn paddocks.

You travelled with me back to Wellington, then Auckland, and finally, onto Sydney. Now look at you, keys yellow as old teeth, type bars slumped in their basket. A hollow amphitheatre. O Brother! Such shouts and applause arose from your chest's alveolus. Letters stamped upon the page as your carriage rolled those sheets away. The bell that sounded the end of each line!

It could have been a boxing match. You returned by sea but too late. Unceremoniously, I dumped you on the side of the road. Amongst stained mattresses, broken TVs, soiled clothing. Then, unaccountably, I wanted to make amends. I returned an hour later, thinking I could salvage something from the past. To mend your broken, metal heart. To assuage my sentimental one. Nothing was found. You had been cleared away with the garbage. A fitting end, brother, I thought. We had both moved on, though not without regret.

YELLOW CHEVRONS

An old story. Our hero wakes up disoriented in a strange and unfamiliar land. Rock strewn, treeless. He is amnesiac; expulsion from Eden is false memory. The Ruskinesque, quartz blaze of a fallen rock. Into his field of vision float half erased memories. The plank hulled ship stretched upon the leek green sea, for instance. Though how did he get here? Balloon cheeked clouds puff powdery gusts from every quarter. The ship tilts toward its destiny, sails pot-belled and proud. An empire in red shading and black lines spell out emptiness. A clutch of minuscule palm trees lean toward the coast. A few towns and oases marked out phonetically in copperplate promise little. Inland remains largely terra incognita, a persistent rumour. He observes a lizard, frozen beneath his shadow, its back patterned with yellow chevrons. This reminds him of ship's anchors. The map fades off, borderless, into obscurity. The horizon swings on its boom in one slow arc either side of the perpendicular. The emissary has not yet returned with news from the ant-headed people. At best, trade routes remain speculative. Twilight is the texture of wickerwork all around him. Soon the stars.

DOMES

A poet was finally selected as the inaugural resident at the W.M. Keck Observatory on Mauna Kea, Hawaii; one of the world's largest telescopes. How was it possible, he asked himself, to write about a universe which, within its vastness, contained no imprint or evidence of human existence? Before him the smoky grey volcanic mountains, the far off glint of the sea, the dense green of tropical foliage, the sharp mountain air and moon-laden nights. The weeks passed. He wrote nothing.

He felt as insignificant as a bellhop in a palatial but empty hotel. 'My words,' he said, 'belong to an outmoded circuitry.' All about him the calibrated machinery of light gathering power. The daunting magnitude of Keck's 'light bucket'. Information became a blur. 'I am as diminished as any one of the million, white dwarfs fibrillating in the heavens,' he cried, 'anything I might write would be as a spectral signature on the ultra-violet.'

Observatory domes, he finally concluded, were the equivalent of the ancient *dolmens, raths* and *duns* contemplating the farthermost quadrants of the *Old Universe*. To map the cobbled ways of star municipalities, long decayed galaxies through fountainheads of gas. The twelve divisions of the heavens. The five zones of the universe; the torrid, the two temperate, and two frigid zones displayed as digital coda, bronze-white on computer screens. Underneath the soles of his feet, he felt the heavy pull of dark matter, echoes reverberating from when the universe first rang like a bell.

TESTAMENT

Goshawk lands upon the glove with the shock of recognition. We have supplanted the God with ego. After that, downhill all the way into invention, great works of art, the ghost of immortality. Sanguine and blinkered attempts to reach past illusion, stave off oblivion. Does anything possess value if we do not bestow value upon it?

O taxonomy of desperation, catalogue of doubt. The imperative that we must not know in order to discover. Humankind's belief system at work. Love, too? The greatest deception of all. The naked self, teetering on the brink of the precipice. Vulnerability meets impending loss.

One man falling off a cliff will clutch at any inaccessible flower in an attempt to stop his fall. That's love for you—grasping at the impossible, hope without foundation. Regret means floating, not falling. Lament also the dismantling of language, lexicon of the poet who falters and fails into obscurantism. That construct wherein ego reigns supreme, declamatory testament to Narcissus, deflected off the burnished shield. Post-structuralists hectoring from Babel's tower drowned in binary codes. In the eye-blink of hawk time accelerates to a still point at the moment of impact.

MANIFEST

There was always doubt that lay indestructible upon the horizon, distant and beautiful in its formlessness, that appeared to be slowly massing but gave no indication of immediate danger. Disturbed and silent as mime yet still too far away to engage us, for it seemed to be a living thing. We could not be certain either way but manned our stations regardless although no order had been given.

The captain remained in his cabin poring over charts. We knew then that cloud had filled the sails, that the horizon had advanced upon us before we knew it, the deck still firm as any foundation beneath our feet, lifting slightly against the cross-winds that carried a sound open to interpretation. A low vibration diminished and faded soon as we felt it. No one could be sure anything had occurred.

There was neither a sense of impending danger nor anticipation only uncertainty. Each man stranded on the leeward side of thought. Each poised at the threshold of his shipmate's imaginings that verged upon revelation but this diminished also. Such was the unknown latitude of our arrested state and collective awareness. The one thing we suspected and later agreed upon was that all shared in this, unknowingly. Some lustrous cloud expanded above the rigging but just as quickly dissipated and was gone. Later, we tried to shrug this off and make light of it. The sea up to its old tricks again, confabulating stories. Even in daylight when the impossible only made its presence felt at night.

BANISHMENT

Compression of car tyres over wet cobblestones at 3AM. Otherwise, dead silence. One street lamplight bore witness. Two car doors cushioned shut. Then the splintering of wood, flashlights, the barking of orders, a scuffle and muffled cries. A cuffed, hooded figure dragged to the waiting 4WD, its engine thrumming. Acceleration. Once more silence descended as the night held its breath.

The poet stood in the dock. The dark suit given him appeared to be an ill-fit much in the manner of a clown. His head shaven yet clumps of hair remained. His expression stoic. One eye squinted intermittently; a bruise encircled it. Clearly, they had made some attempt to confine his vision. This gave him a discernibly startled look. The charges levelled against him were subversion, challenging the literary status quo. Non-compliance. His refusal to accept the terms of his contract invited ostracism and public ridicule.

Fear, that is, vaporized anger seeped through the hierarchical ranks of the literary establishment. The encrypted sentence dispatched from the Tribunal of Heretical Investigation instructed the provincial branches through the Federation of Subscribed Sycophants to deny him any access to official publishing houses within the state, ad infinitum. Banishment. An exile in his own land. But this was nothing new to him except that now this sentence was passed into law.

It was observed during his mock trial that he was distracted though the accusations made against him demanded no response. Nevertheless, he seemed somewhat absent from the proceedings, and if his lips moved, he said nothing. His gaze fixed upon the ornate, wooden coat of arms on the panelling above the bench where his interlocutors sat staring down at him. But he did not see them. His eyes locked on that escutcheon of authority.

A snake coiled around a sword over a daisy chain of laughing children encircling the handle. A beam of yellow light emanating from the head of the snake like a death ray cut a trench around the children at the haft of the blade entrapping them, yet they were oblivious to this in their gay laughter. It was only years later that the samizdat surfaced. A memoir titled: *The Snake Trench and The Children*. A lament for innocence defiled in the womb. There were reported sightings, but nothing confirmed. The poet had long since vanished.

VISITANT

The way perception works its way through spaces, those anticipated, unexpected arrivals. Trust in the acrobatic leap and balance beyond the puppet show of mind. Something recalled but never known through the wormhole of the moment. The curvature of vision captured become multiverse, and you the visitant. Faith, too, in the holding pattern and the focus. Just after dusk when shadows reach out, I will light a candle to greet the night, as time momentarily slows, turns briefly to silence, when thought subsides into darkness as prayer. The ghostly prophet declares, 'Is history a record of the deceased?' Not a question to be troubled by. Especially for the living. Death is merely anonymity. O to escape the confines of ordinariness. 'Habit, habit clogs them dumb'. Speech mutates and fails, all else subsides to shadow. 'Wanted: Dead or Alive' trumpets the apotropaic archangel from the lakebed of deepest sleep.

THE LITERALIST

'Literalists are a bane. Useless, in my experience, to argue with a literalist. I consider literalism to be a perceptual or developmental disability.'—Roger Boyce

His boots were hobnailed with facts and figures, burnished with historical detritus. A man devoid of empathy, a quality which would have interfered with the torrent of commentary and critique governed by a barely disguised self-loathing. A brazen beaver at work building his dam. Such was this self-proclaimed critic, posturing from his virtual lectern in a blog of bombast.

A literary sociopath crouched behind the facade. The clatter of the self-aggrandizing man. He assumed the combative stance of polymath; a Johnsonian behemoth. Refined sensibility was anathema to him, and subtlety he failed to recognize—a dislocation that registered blankly in his mind. Humility was a promise denied him in childhood. He became the schoolyard skulk, surly lipped, and calculated his revenge; all the while that inner voice as leaden echo, 'Notice me! Notice me!'

The years wore on, book critiques accumulated as condescending opinion pieces. Divine afflatus and the ascendancy of poetry remained a persistent mystery, a conundrum that he failed to resolve. The concept was alien to him. Poetry by his reckoning was little more than a mockery of shadow behind rain-blurred windows. Movie reviews were about as close as he ever got to beautiful women.

VIVA LA SANS-DENTS

We broke up cobblestones, just as our forefathers had done, we the 'sans-dents' poor from the sticks, the 'great unwashed.' By the Arc de Triomphe we gathered, stood shoulder-to-shoulder with the 'gilets jaunes' (yellow vests) contingent; were fired upon with tear gas canisters, blasted with water cannon.

At the Champs-Élysées we faced off against police in their black riot gear, shields and rubber batons. For three days fought pitched battles, torched buildings, overturned cars. Some of us fell when we broke through the line, only to advance, and be repelled once more.

An exercise in attraction and repulsion, denial and acceptance, embrace and rejection. One body at war with itself, banners and clarion calls, alarums and flame, our bodies barricading one against the other as lovers do caught in the death struggle between love and hate, until exhaustion resolved the engagement.

Ancient battle cries that arose in the collective mind could barely be distinguished from our ferocious breathing—controlled these limbs in some grotesque pantomime. What we enacted would be preserved in memory, that dark hallway down through which time presses, relentlessly.

We observed the bridge between the wealthy and destitute slowly, inevitably collapse, the rich rose on one side of the chasm and the poor, the 'sans-dents' withdrew on the other. The day of conflagration had come, unavoidable and predestined. Each of those pieces of busted cobblestone we hurled in fury served as ostracon, and the casting of our vote.

LADY OF THE MURALS

—Bob Dylan & Sam Shepard / Brownsville Girl

'Out of a headstrong cloud column emerged one square-rigged ship, buckled to the waves …' But here the story neither begins nor ends. "The entire landscape, graveyard, public gardens, Peacocke farmstead over the river, extensively undermined by rabbits," you answered in response to her query about the innumerable burrows, and promptly imagined the whole shebang catacombed with intersections and way stations, a veritable metro-subway system stretching for leagues—Kingdom of the Rabbit.

That smile O how it illuminated her calm, Byzantine beauty. Lady of the Murals. This Russian student, newly arrived to complete her Masters in Mesmerisation. You talked easily for an hour or so then parted. She pointed out that her name, Katerina, had Greek origins, "like the Orthodox Church," she explained. Looking back, across to that trig station in the afternoon light, you observed within its framework a broad, tree-lined boulevard. Dusk, and headlights shimmering off into some other century, already dissolved in space-time, seemingly vanished through the wormhole.

Before walking away you had already taken those farewell steps in your mind, embraced all you perceived of her in that sustained, shared moment. Departure can be understood as symbolic acknowledgement, an inverted greeting yet barely sensed, become footnote to this manufactured recollection. A brief encounter. Beneath the congealed sunset you tracked back to your car, strategically positioned for an unhurried exit, parked there amongst the memorial plaques and headstones.

STAMP MILL

"If that's what it is—we're bleeped!" stated the anchorwoman across the wetlands of CNN. Tweets as bubbles breaking the surface of an aquarium, soft plosives, then nothing. The stopes and drifts of investigative reporting hammered home with stamp mill authority. Visual recognition of white noise. In the other camp, *vox populi*, rigged interviews favoured by the right-wing networks preaching to the blue-collar workers laid off from factories and coal mines, passed over by legislators, while the stringer sounds off on 'Make America Great Again'. He and his crew, wing men to the West Wing, every man jack of them. From desert to red mud country. Once more the world distorts in a hall of mirrors, and denial stunt doubles for truth. But you are here, removed from the clamour. A flotilla of black swans riding at anchor on Lake Karapiro (though more loch than lake) with its drowned village like something out of a J.G. Ballard novel. A handful of bunker and barn style homesteads passed on the way to Little Waipa Reserve turn off. This stretch of lake a quiet backwater, magpies amidst a carillon of pine on the far side. The clear, triple call of California quail, first heard filtering out of the desert in *The High Chaparral* TV series late '60s. Toi toi flares up, bright signal stations. You head back into the city. The day subsides west, cirrus cloud laid out crumpled as tinfoil. Meanwhile, the flat-topped River Explorer, resembling a floating fairground tent, drums upstream on its daily round through peat country to The Narrows.

OTHERWISE

She inhabited that shut down, roller door look. *Clang!* Head slightly bowed, looked neither left nor right, stared obliquely ahead. Her mouth, set like a concrete curb. You caught a passing glimpse as you turned on the roundabout. A stranger going about her daily chores. You thought nothing about it at the time. Maybe she dreamed a life in some Lego Cube house built to resemble a half-opened chest of drawers, opening out onto river views in chain mail light. Supposedly happy in an illusory sort of way but then, to observe is not to judge, so who can say? We take our chances at whatever cost though hardly any of this cause for concern.

In the Land of Otherwise, beware the manipulative hipster *qua* careerist, one who has mastered the art of upfront subterfuge. 'Tis a cove one would not pull into willingly. Unless forced by some barometric pressure drop in the Cycladic trope of the compartmentalized mind. Entirely against one's will no doubt, if indeed such a thing were possible. O wind of ill-intent. Plug your ears with beeswax, lash yourself to the masthead. Pass by traveller, this is no country for old men nor any man. Such hollow, academic dissembling by echolocation may track you down yet. Nothing's lost so what's left to discover? Let such distortions muffle to silence in your wake, Caravaggio of the Industrial *noir* poetic. Success means fulfilling some other need. Gods don't play favourites, all is equidistant. Real life swarms elsewhere.

THE BRASHER DOUBLOON (1947)

Just another day of dames slamming doors. Downtown L.A. Bunker Hill. Once a choice place to live, now a place for those with no choice. Fire traps and dirty tenements. He'd hard-questioned the rare coin dealer who didn't know his time was up. The Western Union Telegram waiting for him back at his Hollywood office bluntly stated, 'Services no longer required.' The wealthy family who hired him to find the stolen Brasher Doubloon lay behind the theft, blackmail and homicides. The body count mounted daily and barely a week on the job. The client's secretary, deranged, terrified of the matriarch, had already fallen for Marlowe and his snap brim trilby. She held the answers as he held her. The temperature dropped before the rain did, then warmed again.

Harbourside city and shot put weather. The living are memories of the dead and dream is the four-poster bed of *Ars Poetica*. Call it by its real name. *The Takedown*. 'O the poverty of the boulevards!' slams in right on cue. Pick any slide show and add your favourite festival. Feels like waiting for either sermon or summons.

The day leaned back like some Robert Mitchum swagger. Any hedge is a maze in waiting, he reasoned. No leads, nothing you could poke a night stick at anyways. A lowering, crumpled tarp of cloud darkened. One slate slab on a blue backdrop. He recalled how Mulholland Dam's curve reminded him of an eyeball though with lopsided, monocular vision. Spillway leaky as a tear duct running from it. He saw the occluded shape at distance in sharp focus under pressure.

GO THE DISTANCE

An elderly lady, wearing shades and head scarf, midwinter, in a bus shelter, looking like a torn down poster, pressed into the corner. Illusory vigilance as you stare once again into the chasm. Look up. Behold the original blueprint unrolled there. A tableau that far exceeds the comet's million-mile tail. Trick or treat, we overburden the balancing scales, upset the apple cart. Go count the spiral galaxies contained within tree rings.

Women's Thai Kick Boxing World Welterweight, elbow jolt, fisticuffs, challenge. The Australian commentator states, "Her face is a horror show." And later, "Her nose is a Picasso." End of round three and the best of five. The Dutch champ chick ahead on points. Skilled in reverse kick to kidneys, knee drop, elbow smash. They go the distance. "Her face (pause) looks like someone's set it on fire and put it out with an axe," proclaims the Australian. His American co-host quips deadpan, "That's very descriptive." Life thumps on. Go count the light years on your déjà vu return orbit.

Here comes the clattering horse drawn caravan, its canvas sides flapping the Last Supper in crude detail, Christ and his apostles jostling in swallowing folds as the travelling players pass through. The whole scene animated in great gulping waves down a tunnel sized gullet. O waste and aridity of deserts! Ghostly footage heading out from cerebellum country. What remains, uncharted territory before the inevitable leap, our faith fallen flat, or by some other leap made, regardless?

THE COMMON GOOD

Reassurances are little more than well-meant falsehoods. 'I do not apologize for the war and subsequent genocide. I did my duty,' wrote the general in his unpublished memoir, marked: EMBARGOED: 50 YEARS. Combat medals and citations testament to his fealty. He had served his country with unfaltering distinction, fiercely defended its corporate, global interests.

The general wanted to be remembered as the bright star who rode high in the saddle. *Inter-Generational Conflict. Mutual Destruction. The End Game.* These represented key chapter headings under the section marked 'Trade Craft'. A tribe is defined by those who oppose it. He argued that this should be strategically interpreted as meaning the military under his command did not condone ownership in the traditional, cultural sense of first nation peoples, but did with impunity lay claim to another's territory in the interests of The Common Good. Non-Negotiable. "History, right there!" he said.

The expediency of a pre-emptive, surgical strike negated calls for restraint or any subordinate opposition to massacre. "Women and children first. Spare no one," joked the General in the company of fellow officers. He scrawled across the 'manifesto-cum-memoir' THE END JUSTIFIES THE MEANS. He is Everyman. Axis mundi. Earthbound Colossus and Empire Builder. Dream of the Rood. Tree/Cross Incarnate. Redemption and torture. Equalizer in the devil's DNA. Already become monument without a tomb.

White marble. The mountains of Luni. Is the creative act once realized an escape from Self? The pyramidal sea, for instance, wedged firmly in the hill cleft. Burnished. Moon and stars—stairway that fans out into the marble world of Michelangelo. His sanctuary, those mountains. A stage upon which to strut one's stuff. Beseeching dark matter to show itself, waiting for the answer that never comes which, by countless astronomical units, has not reached us yet beyond the Platonic Absolute, the gravelly ring systems of gas giants, over the Blakean convulsions of Jupiter, older than the Big Bang, calibrated by the latest elliptical hula hoop simulations, to give the ghost a skeleton. Does memory of all things exist independently of mind?

We retreat inevitably into the mental bomb shelters of expediency. 21st century cloud banquet retrieves the moment. One Tudor style apartment block newly completed. Ethnicities: subcontinent. Employment: computer programmers and/or gamers. God is dead replaced by Big Data. A driveway bullet-straight leads back from it. Neighbourhood: occasional low life with the eyes of dugongs. Conventional, middle-of-the-road, inner suburbia. A quadraphonic dog barked, chased its DNA, then vanished. Another sunset. This one with deserts flaring in its wake—over storage tanks at Port Jaffa breakwater. Through the *Portara* (Great Door) to the unfinished Temple of Apollo, overlooking the sea on Naxos. Dreams, too, of a worked-out marble quarry, and the sculptor within the enfolding light remembered there.

An impossible conveyor belt of zeros dictate the end of the universe—is nothing something? That we should care when humanity is not there; retrograde, an apology at best, the damage done. So we repeat, and call it history. A parallel universe from the Big Bang (God's hand clenched to a fist), then released. Heavy elements taking flight, a flock of birds to flood emptiness, making of it a contrast, one of our deepest dreams. Nothing escapes, everything haunts. What is gained is lost. We value what must evaporate, destruction in an eye blink—to see, is to know nothing, and nothing is the uninhabited and unknown. We populate doubt, the reservoir of fear with our dreams like lily pads in bloom upon the lake's surface. Beauteous illusions to remind ourselves that we are alive, that we could capture nothingness, to recreate ourselves, endlessly, in this circular argument of life and death. The mind's expansion into nothingness, lost amongst a forest of stars, fording rapids of light, to create a God that does not exist. To remember that each life knows one stilled moment, in totality—is the eternal equation.

THAT FARTHER SHORE

I.M. Rudi Krausmann / 1933-2019

DEAR RUDI, it was following the moon through cloud, that man invented sailing; all invention is mimicry, memory. I heard of your death a year late, forgive me for not getting back to you sooner. The immigrant is, after all, a Colossus astride two cultures; that of his birth, and that of his death. The stance he takes between these two countries is his balancing, around which the winds of change dance, macabre or otherwise.

I have your book of poems, *'From Another Shore'* (1975) before me inscribed, *'For Stephen from NZ Under'*. Given to me soon after I arrived on that other shore late 1986. I open your book and see this from *'Conquests'*: *'6. Don't waste your language on the dead. On the corpses the / systems bloom. / The imagination is imprisoned by its own festival.'*

When we first met, you challenged me. I laughed, and said, "It's okay Rudi, I have blue eyes." I knew that you had been one of the Hitler Youth. It was what your generation did by decree. An Austrian under the German heel. We became firm friends. You said to me once, "Only take from life what you need." Maybe you were right, though life takes more from us than we request, too. That farther shore you have now reached, granted an eternal visa—home at last.

May 8, 2020

JENES FERNERE UFER

Zum Gedenken an Rudi Krausmann / 1933-2019

LIEBER RUDI, indem er dem Mond durch Wolken folgte, erfand der Mensch das Segeln; jede Erfindung ist Mimikry, Erinnerung. Ich habe von deinem Tod ein Jahr zu spät gehört, verzeih mir, dass ich nicht früher darauf reagiert habe. Der Immigrant ist schließlich ein Koloss, der mit beiden Füßen in verschiedenen Kulturen steht; der seiner Geburt und der seines Todes. Die Stellung zwischen diesen beiden Ländern, die er einnimmt, ist sein Balanceakt, um den die Winde des Wandels tanzen, ob es ein Totentanz ist oder nicht.

Ich habe deinen Gedichtband *'From Another Shore'* (1975) vor mir liegen mit der Widmung *'For Stephen from NZ Under'*. Ein Geschenk für mich, bald nachdem ich an jenem anderen Ufer Ende 1986 angekommen war. Ich öffne dein Buch und sehe dies aus *'Conquests'*: '6. *Don't waste your language on the dead. On the corpses the / systems bloom. / The imagination is imprisoned by its own festival.'*

Als wir uns kennenlernten, hast du mich herausgefordert. Ich lachte und sagte, "Ist schon in Ordnung, Rudi, ich habe blaue Augen". Ich wusste, dass du in der Hitlerjugend gewesen warst. Das war deiner Generation so verordnet. Ein Österreicher unter dem deutschen Stiefelabsatz. Wir wurden enge Freunde. Du hast mir einmal gesagt, "Nimm dir vom Leben nur das, was du brauchst." Vielleicht hattest du recht, obwohl das Leben auch mehr von uns nimmt, als wir verlangen. Jenes fernere Ufer, das du nun erreicht hast, gewährte ein ewiges Visum—endlich zu Hause.

Übersetzung: Heinz. L. Kretzenbacher

THE POLITICIAN

The skin is an external nervous system. However, being thick-skinned, that is, impervious to others, the politician failed to notice this. His skin was his armour. Yet those eyes betrayed him, emanating a sense of self-entitlement which overruled any other consideration subservient to that one singular ambition; self-adulation in an accelerated trajectory toward incontestable power. Isolation, for him, meant utter domination over his minions and detractors.

Sleep remained uninterrupted and dreamless. He traversed his daily ambitions negotiating a minefield, every step a caution that left nothing to chance. The day of the great rally had arrived. The crowd was an engine roar. He pressed his palm to his chest beneath the flag. Was his thought faster than the bullet that shattered his parietal plates; did time slow for one nanosecond to register regret for the lies and prevarication, for the statements he believed were for the greater good; did his brain waves spike in that instant seeking escape from the deadly projectile flatlining toward his termination from all earthly obligations; did that thought faster than light allow him one final breath of forgiveness, and if so, was it summarily rejected?

What remained was a public record of iniquities much as expected. The politician reduced to a footnote in history, denied a commemorative plaque. The empire he sought pooled into a halo of blood and bone fragment about his broken skull, there beneath the podium, in the Rose Garden, as cameras whirred and clicked, as his family scattered like a flock of flushed fowl, as security men swooped and dived, as his body twitched one final salute. An afternoon like any other midsummer, a polished sky, the sun deflected bonfires off glass skyscrapers, turned serpentine in the dark shades of his henchmen.

June 20, 2020

ANTHONY KINGSMILL-LUNN (1926-1993)

I am old enough now to talk with ghosts—they draw closer.
Beyond the scent of thyme, you saw through pretension, painter
of the Soho School, took me under your wing. You drank me
under the table, one tin cup of Retsina after another on Hydra,
refuge for painters and poets, musicians. You invited me back to
your villa, fifteen minutes from port along the coast to Kamini, at
the top of the gully. Your partner at the time, so much younger,
silent mostly, wan, a Pre-Raphaelite beauty, said to me, "Watch
this." As she prodded you out of your drunken stupor. How you
growled and snapped awake. Maybe a cruel party trick for
houseguests, who can say? Brilliant, delicate painter, acrylics and
watercolours, a disciple of Cézanne, who captured that silvery
light, the glowing whitewashed villas, so long ago. You told me
'grey' was the most elusive colour in nature. Would you have
observed that the underside of a leaf is cloud coloured?

And trust, too, where you likely trusted no one. An original,
first edition of your friend the poet, George Barker, inscribed and
signed, you lent me to read, which in your absence I returned via
Bill's Bar where we often met, prior to my departure. A return to
Athens, briefly, then the Magic Bus to Salzburg, thence on to
Vienna to fall in love, but that road lay some weeks ahead. Every
poem is a letter to the lost and abandoned, those guardians of
memory, of pain and loss. Even then, I sensed I would salute you
years hence, where your ghost lay in wait. Hydra, those women
who would take you, and take you into them, meant a shared
moment of nothingness, pleasure for its own sake without
meaning.

How distant it all seems now—a dream; failed expectations,
evaporations. You would have embraced mediaeval science that
saw 'vision as light "dwelling" in the eye.' I heard you had died in
poverty (a clochard on the streets of Paris), in London, the
summer of 1993. That City of Light where you once studied at

the École de Paris, telling tales of your friendship with Leonard Cohen for money and drink—where was your friend then who might have come to your aid, though likely your pride would not have allowed it? Anthony, rest easy in whatever ring of moss that now encircles you. True artist, a man who accepted me on trust alone.

September 18, 2020

THE PRINTER

for John Denny

There is something military about letterpress machines. They sit stolid and grounded, quiet as field guns in the no-man's land of the imagination, tempered and trained to respond under the guiding hand of the printer. Type selected and balanced upon fingertips, set letter by letter, word by word.

Press of the lever on quality cream paper stock. Conclusive, repeated click of machinery wheels. It speaks its own language. Meanwhile, the world outside the printer's shed hums and computes its obscurantist algorithms, oblivious to the press and bite of type, page after page.

Spring unfolds, hand stitching leaves to trees. What is it heard here, felt within the breath of machinery steadfastly at work, but the concordant and forgotten dialogue of horse hooves and carts over cobbled ways, rain punctuating slate roofs, a distant bell ringer, the lighting of gas lamps.

But then there is the slightest, barely audible hush of paper sheets that grow and gather into a stack, an exhalation of the printing press, telling of creaking sails at the inlet, faint piano notes issuing from an upper room of some long-lost village manor, fingers turning the newly printed page—while elsewhere, in dingy attics, the proclaimed manifestos of poets, artists, revolutionaries.

DIGITAL GHOSTS

On the decimation of World Literature
extirpated from the NZ National Library.

The sparrow and the bumble bee—the pea-green boat is the mandarin tree. Bumble bee with a full hull, drops down, turns starboard. One sparrow. A shadow. One sparrow, singing 'threepence' repeatedly, hammering a piano key, flashing inside its head. On to the next branch. Closer. Not a tweet.

You could be looking from a cherry picker right inside that tree. The song remains the same. You think about that for a bit by which time it's gone. 'Minutiae' calls the blackbird announcing dusk. I agree, the whole thing shut down. Rain, steady as a slow train passing. 'She wants to be pretty, she wants to be liked' you surmise of the couple passing by the other side of the wooden fence.

Can an incident avoided yet be an introduction or is it nothing other than the crossing of boundaries? The truck and trailer units arrive under cover of dark. Shadowy figures lifting crates of books off the landing bay into the containers to be shipped out like overstayers. Scanned, then dumped into a mass graveyard of second hand bookshops or remote warehouses in the Mojave Desert under lock & key.

Hear the muffled voices subside into dusty silence. First editions become coffins for the voices of long dead authors. Two dimensional entities wailing round forlorn mesas and through the empty shelves. Digital ghosts extracted from the printed page, reduced to the muted babble of tongues, and memory the last, fading note of the songbird, dissolving in the twilight at the end of an era.

October 31, 2021

FARTHER OFF

Tesserae of Suffolk sheep. Even at this angle, difficult to count. A handful at best—the paddock opposite the cantilevered cranes, foundational, iron-caged reinforcing, yellow and orange tip trucks strewn about the riverside, a child's overturned toy box. And I, on the other side here at the lookout, river sweep indifferently flexing past. Bridge span under construction, slowly falling into place. And I, seeing the whole thing through time-lapse photography. The Meccano methodically assembling. Autopsy in reverse.

Soon enough, grid-locked houses will arise ghostly as boxed fungi. Diffuse light spillage. One pill-popping moon. Intermittent keyboard of bird species trebling through high wind in oak trees. That is farther off still, can only be defined as memory. Nothing is complete, can only be defined as regret. Hope is absence. It is where one is—isolated on the viewing deck of consciousness threading across plains, deserts and horizons, muffled into mountain passes. Thought envisioned as wild horses in full flight before the footfall of mesas that stud Utah. Cloud rush. Stammer of chopper blades.

BURN DOWN THE AMAZON

Burn down the Amazon. Move the cattle in. Don't worry. McDonald's will buy the meat. Amazon burgers & fries this week's special. Burn down the Amazon. Plant soybean. Shave the land bare. Dig it up. Dry it out. Turn the green and emerald into grey. Who needs it? But what is that gasping you hear, did you imagine it? See how the trees recoil, retreat in shock before the shriek of chainsaws, the ground-breaking growl of bulldozers. Rip down the trunks, they'll reinvent themselves as coffee tables. Burn down the Amazon far as the eye can see, and further still.

What is that pile of ash, was that an indigene's dwelling? Brazil buckles under Bolsonaro's iron heel. Each morning he scrawls in his black book, 'Progress is wealth. Clear-cut trees as far as the eye can see.' *Quema el Amazonas* tattooed on his wrist. But look out! Here come the ghosts rising above the canopy like mist, swarming from the dark. They are deadly. They are silent. They contain memories of all the birdsong wiped clean off the slate— out of the Amazon. Your ears will ring though you will hear nothing within the reign of nothingness. Dead dreams as far as the eye can see, and further still. Taste the dead air. Yes, there is nothing else for it. Burn down the Amazon.

November 27, 2021

FANDANGO

for Nicholas Burns

One bird memories another in a flock of thought, the musicality
winding up in the orchestra pit of trees—pushing around reality
like a Frank O'Hara poetic caper, cavorting in a collapsing
fandango for all or none to hear and see. His breath the suction
and cushioning, close of a studio door, the mind soundproofed,
the poem recorded in voluble breath and sufflation.

Oh how he hopes that nothing is lost or is forever! In the
process of doing so. Such exhalations and dismissals! Those
coloured cubes of words tossed airily, the fusillade of multiple
doubts offset, drowned out, in that cacophonous dismantling the
machinery of language.

Stalactites are the monster cave's mouth, dark tongue
stretching back down the fossilised highway, echoes shaping the
footprints and wall's low hum, forgotten dialogues before the
bone-crack of fire roar, bulk of night sky pushing aside the
snaggle-toothed cave entrance. Read the dictionary of star
wobble watching shadow-stealth. River bed rambunctious water
flow. What proposals by firelight! What exaltations rune at the
back of the skull waiting to be unlocked millennia hence, resting
there bookended by cliff face and lamplight.

December 5, 2021

OBLIGATORY

'I am even disallowed the freedom to be successful.' He had scrawled on the breath-frosty windowpane. Every great perception of any one writer, that transcendent leap—is a trap for another. The still point and revelation. As instantaneous as loss; that which is understood, an invitation refused but, nevertheless, observed. Nothing is ever discarded, abandoned, but seeks safety in the harbour of the subconscious, beyond immediate detection and rides the roadstead, that ultimately of all its failures, turns triumphant.

Again, he scrawled on the breath-chilled pane, 'The endless summer days of my youth. O autumnal relationships.' Nothing lasts. One can only shadow existence. What the object, what the shadow? That there is no God—only endlessness. All else is obligatory distraction. That we live in order to die. 'Explanation is meaningless.' He ghostily wrote. In one recurrent dream he opens the slide doors of an upper story apartment, steps out onto the balcony. Sees the fidgeting lights of the fading traffic flow below, the city under open heart surgery. No need to leap within the confines of failure, yet gravity gripped him as though falling.

OSSUARY

for Gary Mutton

Not quite midsummer. Already, beige, tide rolling hills through January. Bluely, the seismic ridgeline of Pirongia mountain rising into dusk. The river below capturing constellations, continuously, shift downstream. That people are elsewhere, not here—nor within the reach of atmospherics. What happens is expected. Shuttle service of day into night.

Expectation pounces back in time or not at all. How much of this is willed, wishes atrophied or turned to dust. Only small epiphanies remain, preserved within the ossuary of peculiar silence, the other side of every elusive moment. Doubt is always residue, and memory never transformative, an uninvited waiting. So, too, ghosts, costumed and recalled, fleetingly.

He told me how he had disappeared into the state forest. Endless serried ranks of pine. A dream of suburban houses. But for the moment, here they stood, straight as soldiers, staunch guardians. You might conclude, he was the one human wilding amongst them. Maybe the daily carolling of magpies for company and at night, the creak of branches while winds waffled through tree tops, spearheading stars. His reasons for flight largely fugitive, though a necessary escape in his van along the firebreak, then deeper into the forest. At least for now, safely beyond the reach of the harridan. A sanctuary of sorts, isolated, but not lonely.

REBRANDED FREEDOM

An uprooted tree after the storm cordoned off resembles a crime scene. 150 mph wind gusts burgling branches. The harried, noreast getaway. The suburb looking like a shattered bird's nest. The unseen roar all night long. Vision is a reminder, it is an urging.

One white painted statue of the Christ figure standing before the Catholic church, arms spread wide, raised in the manner of a conductor, orchestrating the cosmos, and a world eternally fallen. The seemingly endless flow, a habit of living, the big and small concerns like wagons arranged in a circle about our prospects at any given moment. But all that vanished with the global virus, everyone masked like bandits. No one able to roam the planet freely any longer.

Protests and illegal encampments. Blockades. People lamenting the loss of luxuries once taken for granted. Things not needed considered essentials for comfort. Expediency. Short term demands governed by short term memory. Consumerism as entitlement. A mixed bag of contradictory wants. Banners and flag waving. Contagion of selfishness rebranded freedom.

He goes to one of his two river lookouts. This one by the heritage mansion with its turret. He looks down the bushy slope to the path visible between the greenery. Then over the river, myriad ripples of sunlight passing in stillness. He is never overly bothered—cars parked further on down the road where the kids leap off the pier. But here he is left alone mostly.

The patient river flow emptying his mind. The city beyond the bank on the other side unseen. He sees terraced apartments with glassed in decking. The one remaining old wooden building with its three, snug balconies sitting grandly just below the ridgeline. An invitation to solitude beyond reach.

ENACTED ELSEWHERE

'Because nothing is left,' he wrote, 'myths are reduced to brand names and labels on supermarket shelves. Division the one thing we all have in common. Politicians and priests—spruikers cut from the same cloth.' No aerial bombardment other than what starlight might manage in the countryside. Meanwhile, within the city, concrete barriers remain in place. The barbed wire leer of the protestors on the other side confronting the police line. Slogans and banners of conspiracy theorists. The endless wait for something or nothing to happen in the push and pull of anger.

Even under the variegated English elm in the public gardens. Or any other tree in its pool of shadow. Exercising his eyes over the flickering leaves, and stillness all around him in the greenness held like a secret. Memory is a riot enacted elsewhere. Then there is that other emptiness, the cacophony of hurt though not recognized as such, buried within the panacea of pettiness or distraction rising to a kettledrum clash and crescendo. But nothing is heard in the muted clamour of the crowd. In the imagining of it.

And then he remembers the dawn walk up the mountainside from the harbour cafes and bars below on Hydra. Everything emerging—from a negative slowly coming into focus. The Norwegian pointing out to him the grainy rust stain from the guttering running down the whitewashed wall, its crystalline translucence, something only a Scandinavian would first notice, something that Tomas Tranströmer delicately netted time and time again.

PHANTOMS

The smallest things are not only acutely perceived in detail but amplified in loneliness. We are each of us a universe unto ourselves. The lone poet, seeking himself out, lonesome, in company—is both a hiding and an escape. Oft-times wrapped in the safety of some far-flung recollection. Colourful stills from childhood. Youth's mosaic. The lost wonders.

A late summer afternoon coming home from school, my mother lying on a blanket, face down on a pillow, asleep, in the angling sun. A woman's magazine and Capstan Plain cigarettes nearby. 'Out-the-back' of our Karepa Street home, by the weatherboard bach, next to the passionfruit vine that never fruited, strangling the slumped summerhouse with an old park seat no one ever sat on. Stillness of the declining day with the sun heading westward. Backdrop to the ramshackle hen house and run, its few peach trees gone to wood, then further back still to the towering macrocarpa, where the morepork called softly from the top of the tree late into the night, though never seen. All of which no longer exists. Phantoms materializing on the photoplate of memory.

LETTERS TO THE LOST

DEAR LEIGH, The magpie warbling of this galaxy that contains us; maybe you have heard it too, being proximate, within the eternal moment, forever in transit, eternally. I wonder, do you look back at your departure from this planet, blue as an eyeball, peering back into space, unblinkingly? I felt your passing by, our lives as we lived it together back then, caught you at that moment, harmonious, or so it seemed. A refined and fragile endowment to my sense of it, of you, present in passing. Who can say, if this was memory engendered by age, another journey into the future—both of us in transit; can one recapture loss as vision? Even these thoughts appear to be letters to the lost.

And then I see you. Remember your eyes burning bright as lamps, pleading to bond with you in marriage. Yearning for childbirth, you lying beneath me—though a too young marriage I had recently fled from, not wishing for another. How alive you were in your bodily pleading! Your brother dead at twelve from cancer. Victim of deadly insecticides your father cast over his crop farm. The same cancer that would claim you years hence, in your early forties, London based for the second time, after your schizophrenic breakdown from which you had recovered. Finally laid low, as if pulled back to your East Coast childhood home. The embodiment of your spirit arisen in your full blooded, bright-eyed laughter, as you passed me by.

THE BIG BLUE BULL

Lullaby for the School Children of Te Kuiti, King Country

Summer had shut its door. The CABBAGE TREE looked around and saw autumn peeking over the fence. Cabbage Tree looked into her wardrobe for warm clothing. There was a heavy green cloak made up of flax leaves, and a pair of moss gumboots. She took off her pearl necklace, because that was for spring and summer, and put them away for the warmer weather. She asked autumn (her new neighbour), 'Now, what can I wear for these oh so very cold days, do you have any suggestions, you have such a warm and colourful wardrobe?' Such was the Lament of the Cabbage Tree.

The BIG BLUE BULL rampaged down Rora Street. Tall as a two story building. Its coat was fiery blue and glittered with a metallic light. Its hooves were black and glossy. Black as bitumen. Its eyes shone red as bonfires and flashed quick as police sirens. When the Blue Bull roared, all the gorse jumped on the hills that rose over the town. Sheep tumbled off hillsides into gullies. *Toi toi* did a Mexican wave. When it sneezed, bushes and trees thrashed back and forth in a stormy sea of green. When the Blue Bull stomped its hooves, sparks flew up into the sky, cinders flung from a bush fire.

It's horns were ivory white and big as elephant tusks. The townsfolk hid behind closed doors and drew the blinds as the Big Blue Bull stomped south down Rora Street. Buildings bounced and swayed. Roofs rattled. Train lines curled and buckled and lifted and fell. Train carriages shuffled and squeaked and clanked. At South End, Rora Street, The GIANT SHEARER on his pedestal slowly woke up, and stared whitely into the light.

The ground shook and grumbled as the Blue Bull advanced further down Rora Street. For more years than anyone could remember, the Giant Shearer had leaned over his stone sheep forever fixed in the act of shearing. Motionless. Bent over that stone sheep through wind and rain, hail and fog. *His back hurt.* The Blue Bull stomped and roared and stormed down Rora Street. He tossed his head this way and that. His curved ivory horns flashed in the sunlight. He moved closer. The Stone Shearer, stretched, stood upright. He looked that Blue Bull straight in the eye, then coughed, froze him right there in his tracks, rock solid.

AN AWAKENING

A perilous fall into the claustrophobia of self-hood, 'undisciplined squads of emotion', the tunnel collapsed, oxygen of the overturned gaze diminished and stifled—ego withdrawals banging its head against the wall of nothingness, and darkening. This could be a dream, wherein you sense no escape, an astroid of broken realities hidden in daylight, caught in the convection current of dreamscape, around your dimming fires, deepening into sleep. Barriers muffled, an awakening toward that distant horizon not yet arisen. Mind throttled curtains hushed.

Awoken, the incomplete script tossed aside—the stage abandoned. Freedom of light over the rim of a camellia bloom, in April, gently tremulous, holding the secret of ever diminishing silence—the moon pushing to fulness, fixed as a candle flame, haloed. That chance leap into consciousness is vulnerability. The steady stare upon Self where every enquiry eclipses to doubt. All things repeat, as we depart into the great objectivity of the Techno Age, the final loss before the beginning. No God. No aliens. An apology for all our designed destruction, heaped upon each and everyone of us, is a compilation of histories long since buried.

SPUN FREE

A neon-lit cross, atop a Catholic Church, wafer-thin, slotted, burning on the tongue of memory. But this, more recently, was at an intersection's red stop light—straight ahead of me, not behind in the gorse bush of youth, nor before. The visual rising up front was a balancing act, not the revelation of some abandoned faith rubbed clean from the door mat of recollection.

St Joseph's, Mt Victoria, for instance, back down from the Hataitai Tunnel, darkened and gasoline polluted, its cataract oval exit seemingly ever retreating, dimly distant—but here, my mother would often take her children (or those of us yet the youngest) to Sunday Mass, as she enjoyed the Polynesian church choir celebrated for their harmonious, though gentle outpourings, and vibrant traditional dress.

Somewhere, maybe, on the other side of that tunnel, lurked the '60s and the freedom of my teens that awaited, once I'd spun free of a Floyd Cramer album and 'Good Vibrations'. Wellington days and Brooklyn Heights. 'Our father' heading toward an early grave, laid low by his lost faith in a socialistic humanity, relentlessly assisted by cheap booze. 'It was the best of times, it was the worst of times' I recalled, as the lights changed back to green, and I swung away.

FLICKERING COMPASS

We live in an Age known as the De-Truth Syndrome. Mediocrity replaced honesty, which might be loss, the ego as ambush. What freedom lost? What hope forgotten? Boundaries blurred, distances dissolved. Compass of the spirit broken, disrupted by invisible forces that defy individuality; chaos indeterminate and boundless. Whatever the lie foretold now empowers—as if some universally confirmed disbelief assumed the mantle of immortality.

I think then of those trees, in the half-hearted darkness, thrashing in the spirit of autumn, shedding leaves, and the colour-fraught beauty of that gesture alone, as if nothing were truly lost. This is not the question posited here. Rampant self-delusion now become the acceptable convention, abandoned unto the forces of negation; the flickering compass, the point of no return.

As if transported back into some neolithic cave art. An ill-disclosed dream, fully represented amongst fluctuating shadow-recall and wall contour; prophecy of belief seemingly unknown, intimated within this contained silence. Breathless, that rhythmic perspective dissolving. Hand imprint, fingers spread wide as flower petals in shadow-edged bloom. An awakening, at once fleeting and embryonic, through the slow exhalation of surprise.

April 19, 2025

LYING LOW

Have you heard how a male voice, emphatic yet unseen over some fence line (but then, that too might be illusory), vociferating to his female companion—her answer, pitched (she is close by but her response creates distance between), his deep recall suggestive of brutality, ancient aggression though, simultaneously, an implied protection; possibly directed toward homicidal intent that he is consciously unaware of, reverberates as deep-memory. The fuse unlit in his erstwhile existence, the campfire long since gone cold, those fading embers of his shutdown, subconscious echo. Dreams that emerged in the form of dragons, as if he were the madman of medieval forests—an arboreal archetype, the primal Merlin. Nevertheless, lying low, waiting to ambush, to reignite the fuse and pounce though, at this very moment, he is unaware of the demons that swarm within, struggling to break the surface from ancestral consciousness. Unaware that even the smallest flare might release a conflagration of fury, the lineal calm finally severed; and she, too, fallen silent before his sensed recognition, the continuum ever present though lost, somehow seeking intent while, relentlessly, fading in-and-out of his submerged premonition as ghost-shadow.

HERMIT'S CELL

DEAR BRETHREN—I humbly address you today as one who has departed the faith, or perhaps my faith has abandoned me! Either which way, I am caught between wrack and ruin. When I look at the tabernacle all I observe is a sealed closet, as if, in my confirmed doubt, I find myself confined within, unable to escape, given that my personal sanctity has since withered to nought. Pensively, and from my hermit's cell, I see a car-tyre swing hanging from an old oak tree by the forgotten farmstead. Hammock-like paddocks roll distant, stalked by pylons striding off toward the horizon. Early autumn. Faintly trill the cicadas. Elsewhere, farther off and unseen, a river passes by under patches of sunlight.

I pray that you forgive me, for I digress. Back in the day, I trained to become a Catholic priest, but threw in the cassock as a bad job, and then as a painter of minuscule, illuminated icons, saintly subjects on small cards, as if I wished to shuffle the deck for the Good Lord. Each one a Hail Mary to the banished God— and so I say unto you, O ye of little faith! Welcome to my eclipsed world, friendships cut short on some assumed pretext, failing to meet enforced, puritanical expectations; I am an island unto myself.

The God I thought I knew now retreated beyond the outer reaches of the cosmos, taken eternal refuge before the altar of the Big Bang. His first great resounding, self-congratulatory hand-clap for creating us as imperfect beings. Then came evolution. Oh, but I hear you cry, 'How can the perfect God create an imperfect hominin species?' A Christian response to that conundrum, brothers, is as we all know—*we were given free will so we could choose!* In that very sophistry resides little choice. It is an ultimatum disguised as redemption. Brethren, I now stand before you, friendless, both as failed painter and defrocked priest. We were born alone and we die alone. I seek sanctuary in the Land of the Ordinary. Amen.

LAKESIDE

A long, moody gravel driveway cuts up into the hillside to some otherwise, invisible homestead, or so I imagined. Trees had turned into autumn lamps as I headed along the far side of Lake Karapiro, stretching thinly away into the distance, and bright as tin.

Midway, driving lakeside, and a near-confrontation on a one-way bridge. An opposing car racing to claim access, though I was first to enter—both stopped opposite ends facing off, as the other flashed headlights full beam at me. So I reversed back out, giving the driver first option, as the car steadily accelerated toward, and then sheered straight on past me, without so much as either a hand-wave—not even the slightest acknowledgement.

I felt an overwhelming sense of something quite sinister issuing from that departing driver who, stony-faced, stared straight ahead during the passing interception. For the continuation of my journey, this partly unsettled my reverie. I wondered, had I simply imagined what I felt here in this quiet location. A sanctuary of sorts.

I sought that which is the absence of what I do not know—an emptiness awaiting surprise. The slow pump & reflex of leafy trees, flickering in a breeze; is this then, as claimed by some, the advent of duende? No god will answer to appease, no ancestral memory will arise. Thankfully, this released me from obsessing over negative speculations which for a time pursued.

GRAND REHEARSAL

'The terror of the virgin page.' Didn't Dylan Thomas say something similar? That sheet of paper flat as any snow covered plain. The boisterous noise of nothingness. A voyage not yet undertaken—the country of the mind undiscovered. Time stands sentinel and awaits your command, before the barbarian onslaught of destruction ensues and sleep, inevitably, prevails. Land of the Lost in the jumbled web of dreams where nothing triumphs. Though you awaken with the ghosts pulling at the hem of your consciousness. Regardless, all that fades. Is this the last grand rehearsal for the 'Big Sleep'; *the endless, and ever extending moment*, enacted through multiple retakes, without any supreme director?

What awaits is nothing other that cannot be extracted from the rubble of guilt and wished-for conquest. Dreams on auto-pilot, in mimed repeat, like so many stuttering machine gun salvos, over and over, relentlessly spilling into that forever diminishing void. There is neither conclusion nor resolve; this is ever present, no matter what awaits—hopefully, gravity, and the dominion of one more emergent day. But this presupposes you had returned or at least, have not yet passed through the Godly Corridor of the Landless, into the customs checkpoint of acceptance or rejection that lies ahead. Dreams, those haunted expectations, under-current of all our past and collective histories, fragmented, and of those yet to come.

HIS BELIEF

In celebration of David Attenborough's continuing commitment to environmental concerns on this planet and reaching his 100th year.

DAVID ATTENBOROUGH, custodian of this orb, guardian of the planet, defender of the oceans—at ninety-nine years of age, his mind undimmed, relentless, surprised still, as if he held the secret to eternal youth. His life a prayer of thanks and gratitude for the forests, lakes, mountains and rivers, for the birds and fauna of our embattled planet. His relentless demand for the preservation of every threatened species barely extant throughout the world's noosphere. His forthright hope upheld and stalwart, never faltering under the threat and flux of fortunes.

I imagine him in the light of a 9th century, Anglo-Saxon king from Wessex residing there in his bow-sided, long house dwelling with its hog-backed, straw thatched roof, woodsmoke spiralling out into the dewy air—envisioning the future as yet unrealised and therefore under continuous, and ever present threat, to be forcefully defended within his dreamscape. As if continuously looking back, driven compulsively to sustain his fundamental belief in this primal earth. To retrieve its ever diminishing echo from fading away into oblivion. Some visitant setting forth on a promised mission to ensure the health of the world's oceans essential to all living things. That is his legacy and the wished-for world he bequeaths us.

A NOTE ABOUT THE AUTHOR

Stephen Oliver—Australasian poet of seventeen poetry collections, seven chapbooks, and one memoir. Travelled extensively. Signed on with the radio ship *The Voice of Peace 1540 kHz* broadcasting in the Mediterranean out of Jaffa, Israel in the late '70s. Free-lanced in Australia/New Zealand as *production voice, narrator, newsreader, radio producer, columnist, copy and feature writer*, etc. Lived in Australia for 20 years. Currently living in NZ. He has published widely in international literary journals. Regular contributor over a twenty year period of creative non-fiction and poems to *Antipodes: A Global Journal of Australian/New Zealand Literature*, USA. Poems translated into German, Dutch, Spanish, Chinese, and Russian. Represented most recently in the following: *Writing To The Wire Anthology*, edited by Dan Disney and Kit Kelen, University of Western Australia Publishing 2016; *The Australian Prose Poem Anthology*, edited by Cassandra Atherton and Paul Hetherington, Melbourne University Press 2020; *Te Pūrere* /(The Getaway) *Anthology* of ex-pat kiwi poems, edited by Vaughan Rapatahana / John Gallas, Cold Hub Press, Christchurch 2025.